Malicious URL Detection - Introduction

Dr.N.Jayakanthan

ISBN 978-93-5610-541-6

Published in India 2022 by Pencil

Contributors:
Editor: Dr. N.Jayakanthan

A brand of
One Point Six Technologies Pvt. Ltd.
123, Building J2, Shram Seva Premises,
Wadala Truck Terminal, Wadala (E)
Mumbai 400037, Maharashtra, INDIA
E connect@thepencilapp.com
W www.thepencilapp.com

Author biography

Dr.N.Jayakanthan is an innovative teaching professional who strongly believes in being a catalyst in the learning process. He has 20 years of teaching, 10 Years of research and 3 years of Industrial experience. He holds a doctoral degree in Computer Applications from Bharathiar University, Coimbatore. He has strong knowledge of subject areas in Computer Science combined with a broad subject background, Well versed in teaching subjects like Data Structures, Algorithms, Unix/Link, Software Testing, Networking, Python, C , C++, XML , C# .Net, Java.

CONTENTS

1. Introduction.. 6

1. Introduction

Malicious URL detection a state of Art survey

Web applications are the essential component of human life. People carry our various operations including e-commerce and online banking. The web security is a major issues in the current scenario. So it essential to detect the malicious URLs of the phishing website. It is light weight approach and prevents the user from those websites. This survey analyzes various malicious url detection method and provide a road map for new research in this area.

Introduction:

Detecting malicious URL is an essential task. The proposed method analyze various features , data collection method and classification techniques.

Bhagyashree E. Sananse and Tanuja K[6]. Sarode proposed feature based approach to classify the malicious URLs. Lexical features, WHOIS features, PageRank and Alexa rank and PhishTank-based features for classification. Web mining heuristics on Random Forest algorithm is used to classify phishing URLs. S. Carolin Jeeva and Elijah Blessing Rajsingh[10] analyze the features of the URL using associative rule mining algorithm. The features are transport layer security, unavailable top level domain in the URL and keyword in the path token of the URL were found to be sensible indicators for phishing URL. A. Le et al[41] obtain new lexical feature and heuristics algorithm to protect against the attack.

Fuqiang[8] Yu proposed A malicious URL (Uniform Resource Locator) detection method based on BM (Boyer-Moore) pattern matching method. This method compares URL source code with the virus characteristics in the database to classify the URL is genuine or malicious.

A malicious URL detection using instant messaging is proposed by D.J. Guan et al[21]. This method analyzes the anomalies of URL messages and sender's behaviour. Malicious behaviours are clustered in several behavioural patterns. It identifies the malicious features of the URL. This method is not accurate in detecting malicious URLs.

Marie Vasek[46] et al perform an analysis a blacklist based approach which detects the malicious URL. It concludes more exploit kit such as black hole and styx are more to be blacklisted and paid services are more effective in classifying malicious URL than the free services. Machine learning approaches are used to generate the black list[66][65]. To overcome the black listed methods the attackers are generating malicious URL using various algorithms. It contains alpha numeric form.[70]. Detecting malicious URL in right time is significant task to prevent the user from various cyber attack[67][11]

Ram B.[57] Basnet proposed new search engines, to reputation, and statistically mined keyword based features for classifying phishing URLs. They used supervised learning methods for classification. This approach detect the phishing URL effectively.

Himani Jangra[25] analyzes the search quires using supervised learning algorithm to detect malicious URL. But the search quires are very sort carries inadequate information to classify the malicious URL. Monther Aldwairi and Rami Alsalman proposed a method to detect malicious website using lexical and host based feature of the algorithm using Navie Bayes classifier[49].

The URL classification approaches can be classified in to two types. They are static and dynamic approaches. The static approaches analyze the URL features for classification. The dynamic approaches analyze behaviour of the URL for classification. S. Chhabra et al[12] identified a method to protect malicious URLs. The short URLs are used to hide the malicious URLs to carry out phishing attack. The short URL services to providers rely primarily on blacklists to stop]generating malicious URLs[44][23][4].

Malicious URL Detection

Dynamic Approach

Static approach

Figure 1 Types of Malicious URL detection methods

2. LITERATURE REVIEW

2.1 Static Approach

The static approaches are feature based approaches. They analyze the various features like Lexical features, WHOIS features, Page Rank and Alexa rank and Phish Tank-based. These approach analyzes length of the URL, IP address, number of sub domains, ports, words, HTTP protocol,DNS record and PTR record[54][7]. Support vector machine, random forest, KNN, random tree algorithms are used for this purpose[33]. The URL string, Domain name, subdomain, malicious words are commonly used features to classify the URL[37][38].

Support vector machine [SVM] classifier is used to analyze the URL string to detect the given URL is genuine or malicious [58]. Lexical features like Hostname, Primary domain, Path token, TLD, and host based features like WHOIS information, IP prefix, As number, Geographic, Connection speed and Host misc are analyzed using various online learning algorithm. Logistic Regression with Stochastic Gradient Descent, Passive-Aggressive (PA) Algorithm, Confidence-and Weighted (CW) Algorithm. The Confidence and Weighted (CW) algorithm yields high accuracy rate.[34]. Online learning algorithms are simple and easy to learn[71].

Combination of Decision tree and Naive Bayes algorithm[24] [40] is used to classify URL. This method analyzes the HTML features of the webpage pointed by the URL. But this method is a Heavy weighted approach. The entire webpage pointed by the URL is downloaded and the features are extracted for analysis. So this approach consumes more time for classification.

The Support Vector Machine (SVM) classifier is used to analyze lexical, source code and network features of the URL for classification[13]. By using trained URL it is possible to provide a real time classifier. Similarity measure is a significant approach to detect the malicious URLs which is trying to imitate the genuine URL. The visual features are used to calculate the similarity score[3][69][43].

2.2 Dynamic Approaches

The static approaches are feature based approach. But the dynamic approach analyzes the behaviour of the URL for classification. The lexical patterns are dynamically extracted from the URL. The complete Pattern Set algorithm and Greedy Selection algorithm are used to mine the pattern. The extracted patterns are analyzed to classify the URL is genuine or malicious[16].

The K-Mean clustering and Navie Bayes algorithms are used to detect the dynamically changing structure of the URL[31].The URLs which attempt to install the malware through advertisement in the client system are analyzed and detected based on their behaviour[55]. Behaviour based analysis are used to detect the spam URL. The behaviour analysis is used to detect malicious URLs in social media. The behaviour signals of how the links are posed and how they are accessed are used to classify the URL[9]. The spammer behaviour are analyzed.

The malicious URLs in twitter stream is detected by analyzing the redirection pointed to same servers [59]. Another approach analyze log file generated after URL is clicked using machine learning algorithm for classification

[52]. The source codes of the URL and the malicious functions in the database are done the pattern matching through the analysis of the finder downloading the source codes so that the malicious URLs can been detected [19]. The behaviour of user and the URL they accessed are analyzed to classify spyware[17], Internet Explorer's Browser Helper Object (BHO) and toolbar interfaces to monitor a user's browsing behaviour [25]. Mitsuaki at al[48] analyze the URL redirection and provide a dynamic counter measure against the malicious URL redirection. G. Stringhini et al analyze the redirection chain and produce a redirection graph to identify malicious URLs[64]. Some approaches[20][61] deeply analyze DNS server logs. The information about resource data and access time stamp used for classification. The malicious URLs are used to perform drive by down load attacks. It injects the malware in victims computer and exploits they system[15][51].

3. Hybrid Approaches

The hybrid approaches are the combination of two different algorithms to nature of the URL detects the URL. The combination of decision tree and Navie bayes algorithm are used for classification. Malicious URL in the social networking stream is increased today. So it essential to detect the malicious URL in this stream. Lexical and heuristic features are used for classification. The K-Mean clustering algorithm used to cluster the features. Two clusters are formed using threshold value and the system uses the Bayesian classifier to calculate the independent probability and classification of the feature[60].

The various significant feature of URL are analyzed to detect the malicious URL. Two associative rule mining algorithms are used Apriori and predictive Apriori algorithms used to predict the attack through malware URL[10]. Hyunsang Cho[31] proposed a multi-label classification approach RAkEL and ML-kNN used to identify the attack. Another approach analyze URL features using clustering and NavieBayes classification. An automated URL classification techniques which analyze the lexical and host based features of the URL. The SVM and Logistic regression algorithms are used for the classification[1]. The Combination of support vector machine and MD5 classification algorithm are used to detect malicious URL[32][50]. This method analyze the URLs of the search result for classification. M.S Lin et al[42] adopted a a combination of confidence weighted and passive aggressive algorithm to detect malicious URLs.

3. SCOPE OF THE PROBLEM

The approached used to detect the malicious URL are fall into three categories. Static, dynamic and hybrid. The static approach relies on the features of URL like path, domain, sub-domain, special characters and malicious tokens in the URL. The dynamic approach captures the behaviour for classification. Some approaches dynamically extract the lexical patterns for analysis. The third approach is hybrid approach which is combination of two algorithms to improve the classification accuracy. The performance of detection is improved in this method.

3.1 Issues in Static approaches

The commonly used protection technique is blacklisting of known malicious URLs and IP address collected through manual reporting, data sources, honey part and custom analysis techniques. This approach uses various lexical features of URL. This light weight approach is easy to deploy and use. This approach is effective only when one can exhaustively analyze the malicious web site and the update the black list regularly. The drawback is the inability to find the new URLs even if they are malicious. A huge number of false positives are reported due to incorrect analysis. So these approaches should be improved [47]. Another drawback of this method is that it can be slow due to time consuming verification process. The black list approaches[53][8][18] are not efficient in detection. The attackers made few modification in URL to overcome the blacklist. To overcome the limitation of the blacklist based approach the machine learning algorithms are used for classification. The set of URLs are used to for training. Then the algorithm is able to classify the URL is genuine or malicious[67]

Nowadays, the weapon of choice in combat against malicious URL is signature-based approaches. that match a pre-generated set of signatures against the files of a user. These signatures are created in a way so that they only match malicious software. This approach has at least two major drawbacks. First, the signatures are commonly created by human analysts. This, often, is a tedious and error-prone task. Second, the usage of signatures inherently prevents the detection of URL for which no signatures exist. Thus, whenever a new malicious URL is detected, it needs to be analyzed, and signatures need to be created for this threat. After the central signature database has been updated, the new information needs to be deployed to all clients that rely on that database. The signatures are created by human analysts, unfortunately there is room for error[45].

The Lexical features of the URL (URL Length, domain name length , path length and query length) and the Host based information (WHOIS and DNS record) have been demonstrated economically characterising the malicious URL in [35] and partly in[36]. This approach is based on the assumption that the features of genuine and malicious URLs are different. The advantages of these approaches are the ability to classify the website without executing the URL. But the URL classification is challenging task because the new features are introduced in daily as such, the distribution of features that characterize malicious URLs evolves continually.

SL.NO

Feature Type

Example

1

Lexical features

Domain token count, path token count, Average domain token length,

2

DNS Features

Domain name, sup domain , path level domain

3

Network features

Redirection time , domain look up time

4

Other features

IP address Special characters

W. Chu et al[14] calculate the distance metric like domain brand name distance and path brand name distance to calculate the malicious URL. E. Sorio et al [62] proposed method which obtain the header feature from http response header and analyze the age of the header using time stamp value of the last modifier. Few approach classify the URL in 5.5 seconds[72].

3.2 Issues in dynamic approaches

The behaviour based model is dynamically detecting the malicious attack in URL. They also have some limitation. The Finite State Machine (FSM) [28] model uses the various states of the malicious behaviour and they detect the malicious website based on their state traversals. But this approach only detect the attacks based on predefined states(behaviour). This method is not capable of detecting random inputs and new behaviours.

Malicious URL are detected by dynamically mining the lexical patterns[16] of the URL. The complete pattern set algorithm and greedy selection algorithms are used for this purpose. As the size of data set increases, the algorithms running time also increases drastically. So the existing pattern selection algorithms are not delivered a desirable performance, so a better pattern selection algorithm is needed. Dynamic approaches needs sophisticated resources like dedicated servers and virtual machines[39]. The time consumptions also high. The content based features are also used for classification[29][68].

A real time classifier to detect malicious URL in twitter stream is developed [52]. This algorithm analyze machine activity log data such as CPU data usage network traffic and network connection statistics to classify the URLs. But this system is having limitation when the malicious tweets were increased drastically. An SVM based approach[63] to detect malicious URL in twitter stream. This approach gives provision to add and remove the taint URL from the classification list. This approach also having limitation against the emerging attacks when new malicious behaviour is introduced.

Guanghui Liang at al [22] developed a classification technique to detect malware . A dynamic analysis is used to capture API calls and other running information of the malware. Finally a similarity comparison algorithm is used to diagnose the degree of similarity between malware variants. This method is not capable of identifying anti-detection malware.

3.3 Issues in Hybrid approaches

Though static and dynamic approaches yields high performance, they took long time to identify the malicious web pages and tend to miss some attacks like time bomb[27].This approach contain two phases static analysis and dynamic detection , so the model is complex and difficult to adopt new changes. This model requires lot of training before deploying it in real time. For example Cujo a hybrid system for detection and prevention of JavaScript attacks, the detection procedure is repeated for 10 times to report the result. The hybrid approaches increases the performance overhead cost[32]. So the hybrid approaches are effective in detecting attacks. But increase in detection time is the major drawback of this approach.

3.4 Comparative Analysis

The comparison of the three approaches is given below in table 2.

SL.NO

Static Approach

Dynamic Approach

Hybrid Approach

1

Feature based approach

Behaviour based approach

Feature and behaviour based approach

2

Time efficient

Time consuming

Time consuming

3

Cannot detect new threat

Can detect new threat

Can detect new threat

4

Good in analyzing the multipath

Difficult to analyze multipath

Good in analyzing the multipath

5

Manual and automatic

Automatic

Automatic

6

Signature based approaches using black listed profiles.

Machine learning methods

Uses both of the methods

7

Download and analyze the source of the website

Visit the website and analyze the result

Apply both approaches

8

Vulnerable to detect indirect attack

Can detect indirect attack

Can detect indirect attack

9

Low level of false positive

High level of false positive

Low level of false positive

Table 2 Comparison of static, dynamic and Hybrid approaches.

Even though the hybrid approach is a time consuming process, it is efficient in detecting emerging threats with low false positive rate.

4. Analysis of Classification techniques

The traditional approach of classification would involve the analysis and classification of URL using blacklist by a number of domain experts. But this approach is inappropriate because of vast number of malicious URLs available on the internet. Meta classification algorithm is solely based on the malicious words. But this feature alone not sufficient to classify the URL.

The machine learning algorithms are used in most of the existing approaches. The machine learning algorithm has the following drawbacks. Most of these classification algorithm needs big data set. When this classification algorithm is used for a small data set the precision and recall is very low. In support vector machine it is very difficult to update the model to take new data. The Random forest can be unstable because small variations in the data might result in a completely different tree being generated. This problem is mitigated by using decision trees within an ensemble.

K-nearest neighbour (K-NN) classification is an instance-based learning algorithm that has shown to be very effective for a variety of problem domains .The key element of this scheme is the availability of a similarity measure that is capable of identifying neighbours of a particular document. A major drawback of the similarity measure used in K-NN is that it uses all features in computing distances. In many document data sets, only smaller number of the total features may be useful in categorizing URLs.

The feature selection also a challenging task which involves complex computation.[66]. Most of the online learning algorithms depends on huge number of features. Most of the time majority of the features are absent. The big feature set affect the time efficiency of the algorithm[26].

The rough set classification approach provide simplify and clarity in classification. But they are not flexible to all applications and attribute selection [5]][30]. The genetic algorithms also used for classification. But major drawback of this method is that they are very slow[2]

5. Analysis of Data Collection

The various data sources like phish tank, malware database, malware domain list are available for data collection but various URLs are posted by the user and their malicious status are not confirmed[56]. The sample data sources used by various authors are listed in table 3.

SL.NO

Author

Data Set

Description

1

Aaron[1]

UAB Phishing Data Mine

UAB has 9,506 unique domains in its 25,203 URLs (6,114

Malicious.

2

Guan, D[21]

IM conversation logs

It contains URL messages from the network administrator of an anonymous corporation.

3

Da Huang[16]

Fortinet [web-filtering rating engine]

Authors collected 0.5 million labelled malicious URLs and 1 million benign URLs from the web-filtering URL feeds. They also get two datasets from the URL log files: 35000 labeled malicious URLs and 70000 benign URLs.

4

JustinMa[35]

Benign URLs:

1.DMOZ Open Directory

Project

2. Yahoo's directory

Malicious URLs:

1.PhishTank

2.Spamscatter

The four data sets consist

of pairing 15,000 URLs from a benign source (either Yahoo or

DMOZ) with URLs from a malicious source (5,500 from Phish-Tank and 15,000 from Spam scatter).

In Phishtank phishing URLs are either user submitted or obtained via external feeds. The user-submitted URLs are voted upon for verification purposes. Most of these domains came from this data set are community-driven nature. It is slow to remove inactive phishing domains from its feeds[47]. Phishtank is a community-driven site that lives from submissions made by its users. Hence, this approach has the disadvantage that some reported sites may not be phishing sites therefore it is possible that some samples are false positives. Also, note that users were not able to investigate how often phishes reported by Google and Microsoft appeared on phishtank.

The Mark Monitor[45] phishing URLs are obtained from various large e-mail providers and ISPs. To verify them, they are passed through a filter which determines the likelihood the URL is a phishing site. Mark Monitor performs a manual check on the URL which is time consuming process. The lookup algorithm spends most of its time rejecting potential matches. Email address lookup is a two stage process involving first extraction and then comparison of the extracted email against a database containing target email addresses. Extraction of email addresses can be carried out using any conventional method, which typically uses the character set defined by the standards for identifying an email address. So time efficiency is the major issue.

The malicious URLs listed in the data sources contain lot of false positives because most of them are posted by user.

A manual verification is suggested to confirm whether the given URL is malicious. This limitation leads to inaccurate results while used as a model for testing. So to get an appropriate data source is a challenging task.

6. Challenges in the detection methods

Most of the existing methods to detect malicious URL are based their core techniques for a well-known attack. But the attacker invents changes in the existing approach and introduces new techniques. The existing approach rely on the fixed set of features but the attacker make changes in the existing features and also introduces new features. As a result, the detection methods are not able to detect the new attacks. So the analysis and detection techniques needs to be improved. The various techniques like signature based, features based and behaviour based approaches to detect malicious website and contents are facing this limitations due to sophisticated invasions.

Due to the limitations the various existing features are not sufficient to detect malicious URLs. For example we are not able to detect malicious URLs based on the domain name because the attacker frequently changes the domain. Apart from that none of the feature collection techniques are able to collect the emerging features. The existing detection methods suffer a lot from the true and false negatives. So we need a new approach to overcome all these limitations.

The performance is major problem. Most of the detection methods affect the performance of the system. The hybrid approaches consumes bit more time due to their analysis and detection phases. Most of our real time applications are related to various domains such as financial management, health care and etc are time critical applications. So the time efficiency needs to be addressed.

The emerging features, limitation of the detection method and performance are the major challenges in detecting malicious URLs. So these issues are properly solved while designing a new technique.

7. Conclusion

Most of the existing approaches to detect malicious websites are having concrete limitations due to the emerging techniques in malicious attacks. The analysis and detection techniques rely on machine learning algorithms also need to be improved in terms of dealing with evolving features, different feature types, and evasion attempts by attackers. Various static, dynamic and hybrid approaches to detect malicious URLs are analyzed. The static approaches alone are not sufficient to detect the emerging threats of URLs. The dynamic and hybrid approaches opt for the present scenario. The dynamic and hybrid approaches consumes more time for detection. The limitations in classification techniques and issues in data sources are explained. The issues various features and feature collection methods are reported. Our survey provides a road map to new research to solve various weaknesses reported in this paper. Our future plan is to add appropriate features, features selection methods, classification algorithms and methods for data collection to improve the efficiency to malicious web site detection

References

1. Aaron Blum, Brad Wardman,Thamar Solorio,"Lexical Feature Based Phishing URL

Detection Using Online Learning "AISec '10 Proceedings of the 3rd ACM workshop on

Artificial intelligence and security Pages 54-60,Chicago, Illinois, USA,October 08 - 08,

2010.

2. Abramson, David, and J. Abela. "A parallel genetic algorithm for solving the school

timetabling problem." (1991): 1-11[73]

3. S. Afroz and R. Greenstadt, "Phishzoo: Detecting phishing websites by looking at them," in

Semantic Computing (ICSC), 2011 Fifth IEEE International Conference on. IEEE, 2011, pp.

368–375. [58]

4.Y. Alshboul, R. Nepali, and Y. Wang, "Detecting malicious short urls on twitter," 2015.[68]

5. Bazan, J., Nguyen, H.S., Skowron, A., Szczuka, M.: A View on Rough Set Concept

Approximations. In: Wang, G., Liu, Q., Yao, Y., Skowron, A. (eds.) RSFDGrC 2003. LNCS

(LNAI), vol. 2639, pp. 627–630. Springer, Heidelberg [71]

6. Bhagyashree E. Sananse and Tanuja K. Sarode,"Phishing URL Detection: A Machine

Learning and Web Mining-based Approach",International Journal of Computer

Applications,Volume 123, Number 13 ,August 2015. [2]

7. L. Bilge, E. Kirda, C. Kruegel, and M. Balduzzi. EXPOSURE: Finding malicious domains

using passive dns analysis. In Proceedings of NDSS, 2011.[70]

8.S. Bo, M. Akiyama, Y. Takeshi, and M. Hatada, "Automating url blacklist generation with

similarity search approach," IEICE TRANSACTIONS on Information and Systems, vol. 99,

no. 4, pp. 873–882, 2016[44].

9.C. Cao, J. Caverlee, Detecting spam urls in social media via behavioral analysis, in: Advances

in Information Retrieval, Springer, 2015, pp. 703–714.[3]

10.S. Carolin Jeeva and Elijah Blessing Rajsingh," Intelligent phishing url detection using

association rule mining",Journal of Human computing and Information Science",Volume : 6

Number 10.2016.[4]

11.K.-T. Chen, J.-Y. Chen, C.-R. Huang, and C.-S. Chen, "Fighting phishing with discriminative

keypoint features," IEEE Internet Computing, vol. 13, no. 3, pp. 56–63, 2009.[55]

12. S. Chhabra, A. Aggarwal, F. Benevenuto, and P. Kumaraguru, "Phi.sh/$ ocial: the phishing

landscape through short urls," in Proceedings of the 8th Annual Collaboration, Electronic

messaging, Anti-Abuse and Spam Conference. ACM, 2011, pp. 92–101.[33]

13. Christophe Chong [Stanford], Daniel Liu [Stanford], and Wonhong Lee [Neustar],

"Malicious URL Detection".[5]

14.W. Chu, B. B. Zhu, F. Xue, X. Guan, and Z. Cai, "Protect sensitive sites from phishing

attacks using features extractable from inaccessible phishing urls," in Communications (ICC),

2013 IEEE International Conference on. IEEE, 2013, pp. 1990–1994.[51]

15.M. Cova, C. Kruegel, and G. Vigna, "Detection and analysis of driveby- download attacks

and malicious javascript code," in Proceedings of the 19th international conference on World wide web. ACM, 2010, pp. 281–290.[65]

16. Da Huang , Kai Hu and Jian Pei "Malicious URL Detection by Dynamically Mining Patterns

without Pre-defined Elements" International Journal of Word Wide Web. Springer US. Vol

26 Issue 1. 10th August 2013.DOI10.1007/s11280-013-0250-4[6]

17. Engin Kirda and Christopher Kruegel,"Behavior-based Spyware Detection", Proceedings of

the 15th conference on USENIX Security Symposium - Volume 15 Article No.19,August

04,2006,CA, USA. [7]

18.M. Felegyhazi, C. Kreibich, and V. Paxson, "On the potential of proactive domain

blacklisting." LEET, vol. 10, pp. 6–6, 2010[45]

19. Fuqiang Yu,"Malicious URL Detection Algorithm based on BM Pattern

Matching",International Journal of Security and Its Applications, Vol.9, No.9 (2015), pp.33-

44.[8]

20. Grier C, Ballard L, Caballero J, Chachra N, Dietrich CJ, Levchenko K",Manufacturing

compromise: the emergence of exploit-as-a-service". In: Proceedings of the 19th ACM

conference on computer and communication security (CCS); 2012.[49]

21. Guan, D. J., Chen, C.M., and Lin, J.B. "Anomaly based malicious url detection in instant

messaging", In Proceedings of the joint Workshop on Information Security (JWIS),

Kaohsiung, Taiwan 2009[9].

22. Guanghui Liang, Jianmin Pang, and Chao Dai, "A Behavior-Based Malware Variant

Classification Technique", International Journal of Information and Education

Technology, Vol.6 (4).April 2016. pp. 291-295[10].

23. N. Gupta, A. Aggarwal, and P. Kumaraguru, "bit. ly/malicious: Deep dive into short url

based e-crime detection," in Electronic Crime Research (eCrime), 2014 APWG Symposium

on. IEEE, 2014, pp.14–24.[62]

24.R. Heartfield and G. Loukas, "A taxonomy of attacks and a survey of defence mechanisms for

semantic social engineering attacks," ACM Computing Surveys (CSUR), vol. 48, no. 3, p. 37,

2015.[40]

25. Himani Jangra, Chander Diwaker, Atul Sharma," Malicious URLs Detection and

Classification Methodologies ",IOSR Journal of Computer Engineering (IOSR-JCE), ISSN:

2278-0661, PP 25-30.[11]

26. S. C. Hoi, J. Wang, and P. Zhao, "Libol: A library for online learning algorithms," The

Journal of Machine Learning Research, vol. 15, no. 1, pp. 495–499, 2014.[41]

27. HongGeun Kim, Dong-Jin Kim, Seongje Cho, Moonju Park, and Minkyu Park. "Efficient

Detection of Malicious Webpages using High-Interaction cline Honeypots" J. Inf. Sci.

Eng. 28(5).2012. pp.911-924.[12]

28. Hossain Shahriar and Mohammad Zulkernine. "Trustworthiness testing of phishing websites:

A behaviour model-based approach. Future Generation Comp. Syst. 28(8). (2012). pp.1258-

1271 DOI : 10.1016/j.future.2011.02.001.[13]

29.Y.-T. Hou, Y. Chang, T. Chen, C.-S. Laih, and C.-M. Chen, "Malicious web content detection by machine learning," Expert Systems with Applications, vol. 37, no. 1, pp. 55–60, 2010.[56]

30. Hu, Xiaohua, Tsau Young Lin, and Jianchao Han. "A new rough sets model based on

database systems." Fundamenta informaticae 59.2-3 (2004): 135-152.[72]

31. Hyunsang Choi, Bin B. Zhu, Heejo Lee, "Detecting Malicious Web Links and Identifying

Their Attack Types", InWebApps, June 2011[14]

32. Imani Jangra,Chander Diwaker,Atul Sharma,"Malicious URLs Detection and Classification

Methodologies",IOSR Journal of Computer Engineering,e-ISSN: 2278-0661,2015.[15]

33. Jin-Lee Lee, Dong-Hyun Kim, Chang-Hoon, Lee, "Heuristic-based Approach for Phishing

Site Detection Using URL Features " in the proceedings of the third international conference

on Advances in Computing, Electronics and Electrical Technology - CEET 2015,USA,

April,2015.[16]

34. Justin Ma , Lawrence K. Saul , Stefan Savage , Geoffrey M. Voelker," Learning to Detect

Malicious URLs ", ACM Transactions on Intelligent Systems and Technology, Vol. 2,

No. 3, Article 30,April 2011.[17]

35. Justin Ma, Lawrence K.Saul, Stefan Savage, Geoffrey M. Volker. "Identifying Suspicious URLs: An Application of Large-Scale Online Learning". Proceedings of the 26th Annual International Conference on Machine Learning. ACM NewYork, NY USA 2009. [18] DOI:10.1145/1553374.1553462.

36. Justin Ma , Lawrence K. Saul , Stefan Savage , Geoffrey M. Voelker, Beyond blacklists: learning to detect malicious web sites from suspicious URLs, Proceedings of the 15th ACM SIGKDD international conference on knowledge discovery and data mining, June 28- July 01, 2009, Paris, France.DOI:10.1145/1557019.1557153[19].

37.M. Khonji, Y. Iraqi, and A. Jones, "Phishing detection: a literature survey," IEEE Communications Surveys & Tutorials, vol. 15, no. 4,pp. 2091–2121, 2013.[35]

38.P. Kolari, T. Finin, and A. Joshi, "Svms for the blogosphere: Blog identification and splog detection," in AAAI Spring Symposium: Computational Approaches to Analyzing Weblogs,

2006, pp. 92–99.[57]

39. C. Kolbitsch, B. Livshits, B. Zorn, and C. Seifert, “Rozzle: De-cloaking internet

malware,” in Security and Privacy (SP), 2012 IEEE Symposium on. IEEE, 2012, pp. 443–

457.[42]

40.M. Kuyama, Y. Kakizaki, and R. Sasaki, “Method for detecting a malicious domain by using

whois and dns features,” in The Third International Conference on Digital Security and

Forensics (DigitalSec2016), 2016, p. 74.[67]

41.A. Le, A. Markopoulou, and M. Faloutsos, “Phishdef: Url names say it all,” in INFOCOM,

2011 Proceedings IEEE. IEEE, 2011, pp. 191–195.[47]

42. M.S. Lin, C.-Y. Chiu, Y.-J. Lee, and H.-K. Pao, “Malicious url filteringa big data

application,” in Big Data, 2013 IEEE International Conference on. IEEE, 2013, pp. 589–596.

[39]

43.W. Liu, X. Deng, G. Huang, and A. Y. Fu, “An antiphishing strategy based on visual

similarity assessment,” IEEE Internet Computing, vol. 10, no. 2, p. 58, 2006.[60]

44. F. Maggi, A. Frossi, S. Zanero, G. Stringhini, B. Stone-Gross, C. Kruegel, and G. Vigna,

"Two years of short urls internet measurement: security threats and countermeasures," in

Proceedings of the 22nd international conference on World Wide Web. International World

Wide Web Conferences Steering Committee, 2013, pp. 861–872.[61]

45. Manuel Egele , Theodoor Scholte , Engin Kirda , Christopher Kruegel, A survey on

automated dynamic malware-analysis techniques and tools, ACM Computing Surveys

(CSUR), v.44 n.2, p.1-42, February 2012.[20]

46. Marie Vasek and Tyler Moore,"Empirical analysis of factors affecting malware URL

Detection" in 8th APWG eCrime Researchers Summit (eCrime), September 2013.[21]

47. D. K. McGrath and M. Gupta, "Behind phishing: An examination of phisher modi operandi,"

In Proc. of the USENIX Workshop on Large- Scale Exploits and Emergent Threats(LEET),

San Francisco, CA, 2008.[22]

48.Mitsuaki Akiyama, Takeshi Yagi, Takeshi Yada, Tatsuya Mori, Youki Kadobayashi,

Analyzing the ecosystem of malicious URL redirection through longitudinal observation from

honeypots, computers & security (2017), doi: 10.1016/j.cose.2017.01.003.[48]

49. Monther Aldwairi , Rami Alsalman, "MALURLS: A lightweight Malicious Website

Classification Based on URL Features", Journal of Emerging Technologies in Web

Intelligence (JETWI), Vol. 4, No. 2, pp.128-133, 2012. [23]

50. Onashoga, S. A.,, Abayomi-Alli,, A., Idowu, O., Okesola, J. O",A Hybrid Approach

for Detecting Malicious Web Pages Using Decision Tree and Navie Bayes Algorithm",

Georgian Electronic Scientific Journal: Computer Science and

Telecommunications,No.2(48),2016.[24]

51. D. R. Patil and J. Patil, "Survey on malicious web pages detection techniques," International

Journal of u-and e-Service, Science and Technology, vol. 8, no. 5, pp. 195–206, 2015. [66].

52. Pete Burnap, Amir Javed, Omer F. Rana, Malik S. Awan "Real-time Classification of

Malicious URLs on Twitter using Machine Activity Data", Proceeding of the 2015

IEEE/ACM International Conference on Advances in Social Networks Analysis and

Mining.August 25-28, 2015, Paris, France DOI:

http://dx.doi.org/10.1145/2808797.2809281.[25]

53.P. Prakash, M. Kumar, R. R. Kompella, and M. Gupta, "Phishnet: predictive blacklisting to

detect phishing attacks," in INFOCOM, 2010 Proceedings IEEE. IEEE, 2010, pp. 1–5. [43]

54. Prasse, P., Gruben, G., Machlika, L., Pevny, T., Sofka, M., & Scheffer, T. (2017). Malware

Detection by HTTPS Traffic Analysis.published at the Institutional Repository of the

Potsdam University.2017.[69]

55. Provos, N., Mavrommatis, P., Rajab, M. A., Monrose, F., July 2008. All your iframes point

to us. In: Proceeding of the 17th conference on USENIX Security Symposium (USENIX

SS'08). San Jose, CA, USA, pp. 1–15.[26]

56. PHISHTANK. Open DNS project available at http://www.phishtank.com

57. Ram B. Basnet , Andrew H. Sung , Quingzhong Liu," Learning to Detect Malicious

URLs", International Journal of Research in Engineering and Technology, Volume: 03 Issue:

06,ISSN: 2319-1163, June 2014.[27]

58. Romil Rawat Megha Zodape Praveen kataria chandrapal singh dangi," URLAD (URL attack

detection) - using SVM", International Journal of Advanced Research in Computer Science

and Software Engineering,,Volume 2, Issue 1, ISSN 2277-128X, January 2012.[28]

59. Ms. Roshani K. Chaudhari, Prof. D. M. Dakhane ,"A Review on Enhanced Machine

Learning Approach for Detection of Malicious Urls and Spam in Social

Network", International Journal of Advanced Research in Computer Engineering &

Technology (IJARCET), Volume 5 Issue 2, February 2016. [29]

60. Saurabh Muthal,Ameya Pawar, Saurabh Harne,"A Hybrid Approach to Detect Suspicious

URLs",Vol-2 Issue-2 2016, International Journal of Advanced Research and Innovative Ideas

in Education,Volume -2 Issue-2 2016.[30]

61. Schiavoni S, Maggi F, Cavallaro L, Zanero S. Phoenix: DGA-based botnet tracking and

intelligence. In: Proceedings of the 11th international conference on detection of intrusions

and malware, and vulnerability assessment (DIMVA); 2014.[50]

62. E. Sorio, A. Bartoli, and E. Medvet, "Detection of hidden fraudulent urls within trusted sites

using lexical features," in Availability, Reliability and Security (ARES), 2013 Eighth

International Conference on.IEEE, 2013, pp. 242–247.[52]

63.SPOORTHI K ,SARVAMANGALA D R ,"Mail_Alert: Online Suspicious URL Detection of

Tweets from Twitter Public Timeline", , International Journal of Computer Science and

Mobile Computing, Vol.3 Issue.4, April- 2014, pp. 817-824.[31]

64.G. Stringhini, C. Kruegel, and G. Vigna, "Shady paths: Leveraging surfing crowds to detect

malicious web pages," in Proceedings of the 2013 ACM SIGSAC conference on Computer &

communications security. ACM, 2013, pp. 133–144.[64]

65.B. Sun, M. Akiyama, T. Yagi, M. Hatada, and T. Mori, "Autoblg: Automatic url blacklist

generator using search space expansion and filters," in 2015 IEEE Symposium on Computers

and Communication (ISCC). IEEE, 2015, pp. 625–631.[36]

66.Tammo Krueger and Konrad Rieck. Intelligent defense against malicious javascript code.PIK

Praxis der Informationsverarbeitung und Kommunikation, 35(1):54-60, 2012.

DOI 10.1515/pik-2012-0009.[32][37]

.

68. K. Thomas, C. Grier, J. Ma, V. Paxson, and D. Song, "Design and evaluation of a real-time

url spam filtering service," in Security andPrivacy (SP), 2011 IEEE Symposium on. IEEE,

2011, pp. 447–462.[63]

69. L. Wenyin, G. Huang, L. Xiaoyue, Z. Min, and X. Deng, "Detection of phishing webpages

based on visual similarity," in Special interest tracks and posters of the 14th international

conference on World Wide Web. ACM, 2005, pp. 1060–1061.[59]

70. S. Yadav, A. K. K. Reddy, A. Reddy, and S. Ranjan, "Detecting algorithmically generated

malicious domain names," in Proceedings of the 10th ACM SIGCOMM conference on

Internet measurement. ACM, 2010, pp. 48–61.[38]

71.W. Zhang, Y.-X. Ding, Y. Tang, and B. Zhao, "Malicious web page detection based on on-

line learning algorithm," in Machine Learning and Cybernetics (ICMLC), 2011 International

Conference on, vol. 4. IEEE, 2011, pp. 1914–1919.[46]

72. Y. Zhang, J. I. Hong, and L. F. Cranor, "Cantina: a content-based approach to detecting

phishing web sites," in Proceedings of the 16th international conference on World Wide Web.

ACM, 2007, pp. 639–648.[54]

Malicious URL detection a state of Art survey

Web applications are the essential component of human life. People carry our various operations including e-commerce and online banking. The web security is a major issues in the current scenario. So it essential to detect the malicious URLs of the phishing website. It is light weight approach and prevents the user from those websites. This survey analyzes various malicious url detection method and provide a road map for new research in this area.

Introduction:

Detecting malicious URL is an essential task. The proposed method analyze various features , data collection method and classification techniques.

Bhagyashree E. Sananse and Tanuja K[6]. Sarode proposed feature based approach to classify the malicious URLs. Lexical features, WHOIS features, PageRank and Alexa rank and PhishTank-based features for classification. Web mining heuristics on Random Forest algorithm is used to classify phishing URLs. S. Carolin Jeeva and Elijah Blessing Rajsingh[10] analyze the features of the URL using associative rule mining algorithm. The features are transport layer security, unavailable top level domain in the URL and keyword in the path token of the URL were found to be sensible indicators for phishing URL. A. Le et al[41] obtain new lexical feature and heuristics algorithm to protect against the attack.

Fuqiang[8] Yu proposed A malicious URL (Uniform Resource Locator) detection method based on BM (Boyer-Moore) pattern matching method. This method compares URL source code with the virus characteristics in the database to classify the URL is genuine or malicious.

A malicious URL detection using instant messaging is proposed by D.J. Guan et al[21]. This method analyzes the anomalies of URL messages and sender's behaviour. Malicious behaviours are clustered in several behavioural patterns. It identifies the malicious features of the URL. This method is not accurate in detecting malicious URLs.

Marie Vasek[46] et al perform an analysis a blacklist based approach which detects the malicious URL. It concludes more exploit kit such as black hole and styx are more to be blacklisted and paid services are more effective in classifying malicious URL than the free services. Machine learning approaches are used to generate the black list[66][65]. To overcome the black listed methods the attackers are generating malicious URL using various algorithms. It contains alpha numeric form.[70]. Detecting malicious URL in right time is significant task to prevent the user from various cyber attack[67][11]

Ram B.[57] Basnet proposed new search engines, to reputation, and statistically mined keyword based features for classifying phishing URLs. They used supervised learning methods for classification. This approach detect the phishing URL effectively.

Himani Jangra[25] analyzes the search quires using supervised learning algorithm to detect malicious URL. But the search quires are very sort carries inadequate information to classify the malicious URL. Monther Aldwairi and Rami Alsalman proposed a method to detect malicious website using lexical and host based feature of the algorithm using Navie Bayes classifier[49].

The URL classification approaches can be classified in to two types. They are static and dynamic approaches. The static approaches analyze the URL features for classification. The dynamic approaches analyze behaviour of the URL for classification. S. Chhabra et al[12] identified a method to protect malicious URLs. The short URLs are used to hide the malicious URLs to carry out phishing attack. The short URL services to providers rely primarily on blacklists to stop]generating malicious URLs[44][23][4].

Malicious URL Detection

Dynamic Approach

Static approach

Figure 1 Types of Malicious URL detection methods

2. LITERATURE REVIEW

2.1 Static Approach

The static approaches are feature based approaches. They analyze the various features like Lexical features, WHOIS features, Page Rank and Alexa rank and Phish Tank-based. These approach analyzes length of the URL, IP address, number of sub domains, ports, words, HTTP protocol,DNS record and PTR record[54][7]. Support vector machine, random forest, KNN, random tree algorithms are used for this purpose[33]. The URL string, Domain name, subdomain, malicious words are commonly used features to classify the URL[37][38].

Support vector machine [SVM] classifier is used to analyze the URL string to detect the given URL is genuine or malicious [58]. Lexical features like Hostname, Primary domain, Path token, TLD, and host based features like WHOIS information, IP prefix, As number, Geographic, Connection speed and Host misc are analyzed using various online learning algorithm. Logistic Regression with Stochastic Gradient Descent, Passive-Aggressive (PA)

Algorithm, Confidence-and Weighted (CW) Algorithm. The Confidence and Weighted (CW) algorithm yields high accuracy rate.[34]. Online learning algorithms are simple and easy to learn[71].

Combination of Decision tree and Naive Bayes algorithm[24] [40] is used to classify URL. This method analyzes the HTML features of the webpage pointed by the URL. But this method is a Heavy weighted approach. The entire webpage pointed by the URL is downloaded and the features are extracted for analysis. So this approach consumes more time for classification.

The Support Vector Machine (SVM) classifier is used to analyze lexical, source code and network features of the URL for classification[13]. By using trained URL it is possible to provide a real time classifier. Similarity measure is a significant approach to detect the malicious URLs which is trying to imitate the genuine URL. The visual features are used to calculate the similarity score[3][69][43].

2.2 Dynamic Approaches

The static approaches are feature based approach. But the dynamic approach analyzes the behaviour of the URL for classification. The lexical patterns are dynamically extracted from the URL. The complete Pattern Set algorithm and Greedy Selection algorithm are used to mine the pattern. The extracted patterns are analyzed to classify the URL is genuine or malicious[16].

The K-Mean clustering and Navie Bayes algorithms are used to detect the dynamically changing structure of the

URL[31].The URLs which attempt to install the malware through advertisement in the client system are analyzed and detected based on their behaviour[55]. Behaviour based analysis are used to detect the spam URL. The behaviour analysis is used to detect malicious URLs in social media. The behaviour signals of how the links are posed and how they are accessed are used to classify the URL[9]. The spammer behaviour are analyzed.

The malicious URLs in twitter stream is detected by analyzing the redirection pointed to same servers [59]. Another approach analyze log file generated after URL is clicked using machine learning algorithm for classification [52]. The source codes of the URL and the malicious functions in the database are done the pattern matching through the analysis of the finder downloading the source codes so that the malicious URLs can been detected [19]. The behaviour of user and the URL they accessed are analyzed to classify spyware[17], Internet Explorer's Browser Helper Object (BHO) and toolbar interfaces to monitor a user's browsing behaviour [25]. Mitsuaki at al[48] analyze the URL redirection and provide a dynamic counter measure against the malicious URL redirection. G. Stringhini et al analyze the redirection chain and produce a redirection graph to identify malicious URLs[64]. Some approaches[20][61] deeply analyze DNS server logs. The information about resource data and access time stamp used for classification. The malicious URLs are used to perform drive by down load attacks. It injects the malware in victims computer and exploits they system[15][51].

3. Hybrid Approaches

The hybrid approaches are the combination of two different algorithms to nature of the URL detects the URL. The combination of decision tree and Navie bayes algorithm are used for classification. Malicious URL in the social networking stream is increased today. So it essential to detect the malicious URL in this stream. Lexical and heuristic features are used for classification. The K-Mean clustering algorithm used to cluster the features. Two clusters are formed using threshold value and the system uses the Bayesian classifier to calculate the independent probability and classification of the feature[60].

The various significant feature of URL are analyzed to detect the malicious URL. Two associative rule mining algorithms are used Apriori and predictive Apriori algorithms used to predict the attack through malware URL[10]. Hyunsang Cho[31] proposed a multi-label classification approach RAkEL and ML-kNN used to identify the attack. Another approach analyze URL features using clustering and NavieBayes classification. An automated URL classification techniques which analyze the lexical and host based features of the URL. The SVM and Logistic regression algorithms are used for the classification[1]. The Combination of support vector machine and MD5 classification algorithm are used to detect malicious URL[32][50]. This method analyze the URLs of the search result for classification. M.S Lin et al[42] adopted a a combination of confidence weighted and passive aggressive algorithm to detect malicious URLs.

3. SCOPE OF THE PROBLEM

The approached used to detect the malicious URL are fall into three categories. Static, dynamic and hybrid. The static approach relies on the features of URL like path, domain, sub-domain, special characters and malicious tokens in the URL. The dynamic approach captures the behaviour for classification. Some approaches dynamically extract the lexical patterns for analysis. The third approach is hybrid approach which is combination of two algorithms to improve the classification accuracy. The performance of detection is improved in this method.

3.1 Issues in Static approaches

The commonly used protection technique is blacklisting of known malicious URLs and IP address collected through manual reporting, data sources, honey part and custom analysis techniques. This approach uses various lexical features of URL. This light weight approach is easy to deploy and use. This approach is effective only when one can exhaustively analyze the malicious web site and the update the black list regularly. The drawback is the inability to find the new URLs even if they are malicious. A huge number of false positives are reported due to incorrect analysis. So these approaches should be improved [47]. Another drawback of this method is that it can be slow due to time consuming verification process. The black list approaches[53][8][18] are not efficient in detection. The attackers made few modification in URL to overcome the blacklist. To overcome the limitation of the blacklist based approach the machine learning algorithms are used for classification. The set of URLs are used to for training.

Then the algorithm is able to classify the URL is genuine or malicious[67]

Nowadays, the weapon of choice in combat against malicious URL is signature-based approaches. that match a pre-generated set of signatures against the files of a user. These signatures are created in a way so that they only match malicious software. This approach has at least two major drawbacks. First, the signatures are commonly created by human analysts. This, often, is a tedious and error-prone task. Second, the usage of signatures inherently prevents the detection of URL for which no signatures exist. Thus, whenever a new malicious URL is detected, it needs to be analyzed, and signatures need to be created for this threat. After the central signature database has been updated, the new information needs to be deployed to all clients that rely on that database. The signatures are created by human analysts, unfortunately there is room for error[45].

The Lexical features of the URL (URL Length, domain name length , path length and query length) and the Host based information (WHOIS and DNS record) have been demonstrated economically characterising the malicious URL in [35] and partly in[36]. This approach is based on the assumption that the features of genuine and malicious URLs are different. The advantages of these approaches are the ability to classify the website without executing the URL. But the URL classification is challenging task because the new features are introduced in daily as such, the distribution of features that characterize malicious URLs evolves continually.

SL.NO

Feature Type

Example

1

Lexical features

Domain token count, path token count, Average domain token length,

2

DNS Features

Domain name, sup domain , path level domain

3

Network features

Redirection time , domain look up time

4

Other features

IP address Special characters

W. Chu et al[14] calculate the distance metric like domain brand name distance and path brand name distance to calculate the malicious URL. E. Sorio et al [62] proposed method which obtain the header feature from http response header and analyze the age of the header using time stamp value of the last modifier. Few approach classify the URL in 5.5 seconds[72].

3.2 Issues in dynamic approaches

The behaviour based model is dynamically detecting the malicious attack in URL. They also have some limitation. The Finite State Machine (FSM) [28] model uses the various states of the malicious behaviour and they detect the malicious website based on their state traversals. But this approach only detect the attacks based on predefined states(behaviour). This method is not capable of detecting random inputs and new behaviours.

Malicious URL are detected by dynamically mining the lexical patterns[16] of the URL. The complete pattern set algorithm and greedy selection algorithms are used for this purpose. As the size of data set increases, the algorithms running time also increases drastically. So the existing pattern selection algorithms are not delivered a desirable performance, so a better pattern selection algorithm is needed. Dynamic approaches needs sophisticated resources like dedicated servers and virtual machines[39]. The time consumptions also high. The content based features are also used for classification[29][68].

A real time classifier to detect malicious URL in twitter stream is developed [52]. This algorithm analyze machine activity log data such as CPU data usage network traffic and network connection statistics to classify the URLs. But this system is having limitation when the malicious tweets were increased drastically. An SVM based approach[63] to detect malicious URL in twitter stream. This approach gives provision to add and remove the taint

URL from the classification list. This approach also having limitation against the emerging attacks when new malicious behaviour is introduced.

Guanghui Liang at al [22] developed a classification technique to detect malware . A dynamic analysis is used to capture API calls and other running information of the malware. Finally a similarity comparison algorithm is used to diagnose the degree of similarity between malware variants. This method is not capable of identifying anti-detection malware.

3.3 Issues in Hybrid approaches

Though static and dynamic approaches yields high performance, they took long time to identify the malicious web pages and tend to miss some attacks like time bomb[27].This approach contain two phases static analysis and dynamic detection , so the model is complex and difficult to adopt new changes. This model requires lot of training before deploying it in real time. For example Cujo a hybrid system for detection and prevention of JavaScript attacks, the detection procedure is repeated for 10 times to report the result. The hybrid approaches increases the performance overhead cost[32]. So the hybrid approaches are effective in detecting attacks. But increase in detection time is the major drawback of this approach.

3.4 Comparative Analysis

The comparison of the three approaches is given below in table 2.

SL.NO

Static Approach

Dynamic Approach

Hybrid Approach

1

Feature based approach

Behaviour based approach

Feature and behaviour based approach

2

Time efficient

Time consuming

Time consuming

3

Cannot detect new threat

Can detect new threat

Can detect new threat

4

Good in analyzing the multipath

Difficult to analyze multipath

Good in analyzing the multipath

5

Manual and automatic

Automatic

Automatic

6

Signature based approaches using black listed profiles.

Machine learning methods

Uses both of the methods

7

Download and analyze the source of the website

Visit the website and analyze the result

Apply both approaches

8

Vulnerable to detect indirect attack

Can detect indirect attack

Can detect indirect attack

9

Low level of false positive

High level of false positive

Low level of false positive

Table 2 Comparison of static, dynamic and Hybrid approaches.

Even though the hybrid approach is a time consuming process, it is efficient in detecting emerging threats with low false positive rate.

4. Analysis of Classification techniques

The traditional approach of classification would involve the analysis and classification of URL using blacklist by a number of domain experts. But this approach is inappropriate because of vast number of malicious URLs available on the internet. Meta classification algorithm is solely based on the malicious words. But this feature alone not sufficient to classify the URL.

The machine learning algorithms are used in most of the existing approaches. The machine learning algorithm has the following drawbacks. Most of these classification algorithm needs big data set. When this classification algorithm is used for a small data set the precision and recall is very low. In support vector machine it is very difficult to update the model to take new data. The Random forest can be unstable because small variations in the data might result in a completely different tree being generated. This problem is mitigated by using decision trees within an ensemble.

K-nearest neighbour (K-NN) classification is an instance-based learning algorithm that has shown to be very effective for a variety of problem domains .The key element of this scheme is the availability of a similarity measure that is capable of identifying neighbours of a particular document. A major drawback of the similarity measure used in K-NN is that it uses all features in computing distances. In many document data sets, only smaller number of the total features may be useful in categorizing URLs.

The feature selection also a challenging task which involves complex computation.[66]. Most of the online learning algorithms depends on huge number of features. Most of the time majority of the features are absent. The big feature set affect the time efficiency of the algorithm[26].

The rough set classification approach provide simplify and clarity in classification. But they are not flexible to all applications and attribute selection [5]][30]. The genetic algorithms also used for classification. But major drawback of this method is that they are very slow[2]

5. Analysis of Data Collection

The various data sources like phish tank, malware database, malware domain list are available for data collection but various URLs are posted by the user and their malicious status are not confirmed[56]. The sample data sources used by various authors are listed in table 3.

SL.NO

Author

Data Set

Description

1

Aaron[1]

UAB Phishing Data Mine

UAB has 9,506 unique domains in its 25,203 URLs (6,114

Malicious.

2

Guan, D[21]

IM conversation logs

It contains URL messages from the network administrator of an anonymous corporation.

3

Da Huang[16]

Fortinet [web-filtering rating engine]

Authors collected 0.5 million labelled malicious URLs and 1 million benign URLs from the web-filtering URL feeds. They also get two datasets from the URL log files: 35000 labeled malicious URLs and 70000 benign URLs.

4

JustinMa[35]

Benign URLs:

1.DMOZ Open Directory

Project

2. Yahoo's directory

Malicious URLs:

1.PhishTank

2.Spamscatter

The four data sets consist

of pairing 15,000 URLs from a benign source (either Yahoo or

DMOZ) with URLs from a malicious source (5,500 from Phish-Tank and 15,000 from Spam scatter).

In Phishtank phishing URLs are either user submitted or obtained via external feeds. The user-submitted URLs are voted upon for verification purposes. Most of these domains came from this data set are community-driven nature. It is slow to remove inactive phishing domains from its feeds[47]. Phishtank is a community-driven site that lives from submissions made by its users. Hence, this approach has the disadvantage that some reported sites may not be phishing sites therefore it is possible that some samples are false positives. Also, note that users were not able to investigate how often phishes reported by Google and Microsoft appeared on phishtank.

The Mark Monitor[45] phishing URLs are obtained from various large e-mail providers and ISPs. To verify them, they are passed through a filter which determines the likelihood the URL is a phishing site. Mark Monitor performs a manual check on the URL which is time consuming process. The lookup algorithm spends most of its time rejecting potential matches. Email address lookup is a two stage process involving first extraction and then comparison of the extracted email against a database containing target email addresses. Extraction of email addresses can be carried out using any conventional method, which typically uses the character set defined by the standards for identifying an email address. So time efficiency is the major issue.

The malicious URLs listed in the data sources contain lot of false positives because most of them are posted by user. A manual verification is suggested to confirm whether the given URL is malicious. This limitation leads to inaccurate results while used as a model for testing. So to get an appropriate data source is a challenging task.

6. Challenges in the detection methods

Most of the existing methods to detect malicious URL are based their core techniques for a well-known attack. But the attacker invents changes in the existing approach and introduces new techniques. The existing approach rely on the fixed set of features but the attacker make changes in the existing features and also introduces new features. As a result, the detection methods are not able to detect the new attacks. So the analysis and detection techniques needs to be improved. The various techniques like signature based, features based and behaviour based approaches to detect malicious website and contents are facing this limitations due to sophisticated invasions.

Due to the limitations the various existing features are not sufficient to detect malicious URLs. For example we are not able to detect malicious URLs based on the domain name because the attacker frequently changes the domain. Apart from that none of the feature collection techniques are able to collect the emerging features. The existing detection methods suffer a lot from the true and false negatives. So we need a new approach to overcome all these limitations.

The performance is major problem. Most of the detection methods affect the performance of the system. The hybrid approaches consumes bit more time due to their analysis and detection phases. Most of our real time applications are related to various domains such as financial management, health care and etc are time critical applications. So the time efficiency needs to be addressed.

The emerging features, limitation of the detection method and performance are the major challenges in detecting malicious URLs. So these issues are properly solved while designing a new technique.

7. Conclusion

Most of the existing approaches to detect malicious websites are having concrete limitations due to the emerging techniques in malicious attacks. The analysis and detection techniques rely on machine learning algorithms also need to be improved in terms of dealing with evolving features, different feature types, and evasion attempts by attackers. Various static, dynamic and hybrid approaches to detect malicious URLs are analyzed. The static approaches alone are not sufficient to detect the emerging threats of URLs. The dynamic and hybrid approaches opt for the present scenario. The dynamic and hybrid approaches consumes more time for detection. The limitations in classification techniques and issues in data sources are explained. The issues various features and feature collection methods are reported. Our survey provides a road map to new research to solve various weaknesses reported in this paper. Our future plan is to add appropriate features, features selection methods, classification algorithms and methods for data collection to improve the efficiency to malicious web site detection

References

1. Aaron Blum, Brad Wardman,Thamar Solorio,"Lexical Feature Based Phishing URL

Detection Using Online Learning "AISec '10 Proceedings of the 3rd ACM workshop on

Artificial intelligence and security Pages 54-60,Chicago, Illinois, USA,October 08 - 08,

2010.

2. Abramson, David, and J. Abela. "A parallel genetic algorithm for solving the school

timetabling problem." (1991): 1-11[73]

3. S. Afroz and R. Greenstadt, "Phishzoo: Detecting phishing websites by looking at them," in

Semantic Computing (ICSC), 2011 Fifth IEEE International Conference on. IEEE, 2011, pp.

368–375. [58]

4.Y. Alshboul, R. Nepali, and Y. Wang, "Detecting malicious short urls on twitter," 2015.[68]

5. Bazan, J., Nguyen, H.S., Skowron, A., Szczuka, M.: A View on Rough Set Concept

Approximations. In: Wang, G., Liu, Q., Yao, Y., Skowron, A. (eds.) RSFDGrC 2003. LNCS

(LNAI), vol. 2639, pp. 627–630. Springer, Heidelberg [71]

6. Bhagyashree E. Sananse and Tanuja K. Sarode,"Phishing URL Detection: A Machine

Learning and Web Mining-based Approach",International Journal of Computer

Applications,Volume 123, Number 13 ,August 2015. [2]

7. L. Bilge, E. Kirda, C. Kruegel, and M. Balduzzi. EXPOSURE: Finding malicious domains

using passive dns analysis. In Proceedings of NDSS, 2011.[70]

8.S. Bo, M. Akiyama, Y. Takeshi, and M. Hatada, "Automating url blacklist generation with similarity search approach," IEICE TRANSACTIONS on Information and Systems, vol. 99,

no. 4, pp. 873–882, 2016[44].

9.C. Cao, J. Caverlee, Detecting spam urls in social media via behavioral analysis, in: Advances

in Information Retrieval, Springer, 2015, pp. 703–714.[3]

10.S. Carolin Jeeva and Elijah Blessing Rajsingh," Intelligent phishing url detection using

association rule mining",Journal of Human computing and Information Science",Volume : 6

Number 10.2016.[4]

11.K.-T. Chen, J.-Y. Chen, C.-R. Huang, and C.-S. Chen, "Fighting phishing with discriminative

keypoint features," IEEE Internet Computing, vol. 13, no. 3, pp. 56–63, 2009.[55]

12. S. Chhabra, A. Aggarwal, F. Benevenuto, and P. Kumaraguru, "Phi.sh/$ ocial: the phishing

landscape through short urls," in Proceedings of the 8th Annual Collaboration, Electronic

messaging, Anti-Abuse and Spam Conference. ACM, 2011, pp. 92–101.[33]

13. Christophe Chong [Stanford], Daniel Liu [Stanford], and Wonhong Lee [Neustar],

"Malicious URL Detection".[5]

14.W. Chu, B. B. Zhu, F. Xue, X. Guan, and Z. Cai, "Protect sensitive sites from phishing

attacks using features extractable from inaccessible phishing urls," in Communications (ICC),

2013 IEEE International Conference on. IEEE, 2013, pp. 1990–1994.[51]

15.M. Cova, C. Kruegel, and G. Vigna, "Detection and analysis of driveby- download attacks

and malicious javascript code," in Proceedings of the 19th international conference on World

wide web. ACM, 2010, pp. 281–290.[65]

16. Da Huang , Kai Hu and Jian Pei "Malicious URL Detection by Dynamically Mining Patterns

without Pre-defined Elements" International Journal of Word Wide Web. Springer US. Vol

26 Issue 1. 10th August 2013.DOI10.1007/s11280-013-0250-4[6]

17. Engin Kirda and Christopher Kruegel,"Behavior-based Spyware Detection", Proceedings of

the 15th conference on USENIX Security Symposium - Volume 15 Article No.19,August

04,2006,CA, USA. [7]

18.M. Felegyhazi, C. Kreibich, and V. Paxson, "On the potential of proactive domain

blacklisting." LEET, vol. 10, pp. 6–6, 2010[45]

19. Fuqiang Yu,"Malicious URL Detection Algorithm based on BM Pattern

Matching",International Journal of Security and Its Applications, Vol.9, No.9 (2015), pp.33-

44.[8]

20. Grier C, Ballard L, Caballero J, Chachra N, Dietrich CJ, Levchenko K",Manufacturing

compromise: the emergence of exploit-as-a-service". In: Proceedings of the 19th ACM

conference on computer and communication security (CCS); 2012.[49]

21. Guan, D. J., Chen, C.M., and Lin, J.B. "Anomaly based malicious url detection in instant

messaging", In Proceedings of the joint Workshop on Information Security (JWIS),

Kaohsiung, Taiwan 2009[9].

22. Guanghui Liang, Jianmin Pang, and Chao Dai, "A Behavior-Based Malware Variant

Classification Technique", International Journal of Information and Education

Technology, Vol.6 (4).April 2016. pp. 291-295[10].

23. N. Gupta, A. Aggarwal, and P. Kumaraguru, "bit. ly/malicious: Deep dive into short url

based e-crime detection," in Electronic Crime Research (eCrime), 2014 APWG Symposium

on. IEEE, 2014, pp.14–24.[62]

24.R. Heartfield and G. Loukas, "A taxonomy of attacks and a survey of defence mechanisms for

semantic social engineering attacks," ACM Computing Surveys (CSUR), vol. 48, no. 3, p. 37,

2015.[40]

25. Himani Jangra, Chander Diwaker, Atul Sharma," Malicious URLs Detection and

Classification Methodologies ",IOSR Journal of Computer Engineering (IOSR-JCE), ISSN:

2278-0661, PP 25-30.[11]

26. S. C. Hoi, J. Wang, and P. Zhao, "Libol: A library for online learning algorithms," The

Journal of Machine Learning Research, vol. 15, no. 1, pp. 495–499, 2014.[41]

27. HongGeun Kim, Dong-Jin Kim, Seongje Cho, Moonju Park, and Minkyu Park. "Efficient

Detection of Malicious Webpages using High-Interaction cline Honeypots" J. Inf. Sci.

Eng. 28(5).2012. pp.911-924.[12]

28. Hossain Shahriar and Mohammad Zulkernine. "Trustworthiness testing of phishing websites:

A behaviour model-based approach. Future Generation Comp. Syst. 28(8). (2012). pp.1258-

1271 DOI : 10.1016/j.future.2011.02.001.[13]

29.Y.-T. Hou, Y. Chang, T. Chen, C.-S. Laih, and C.-M. Chen, "Malicious web content detection

by machine learning," Expert Systems with Applications, vol. 37, no. 1, pp. 55–60, 2010.[56]

30. Hu, Xiaohua, Tsau Young Lin, and Jianchao Han. "A new rough sets model based on

database systems." Fundamenta informaticae 59.2-3 (2004): 135-152.[72]

31. Hyunsang Choi, Bin B. Zhu, Heejo Lee, "Detecting Malicious Web Links and Identifying

Their Attack Types", InWebApps, June 2011[14]

32. Imani Jangra,Chander Diwaker,Atul Sharma,"Malicious URLs Detection and Classification

Methodologies",IOSR Journal of Computer Engineering,e-ISSN: 2278-0661,2015.[15]

33. Jin-Lee Lee, Dong-Hyun Kim, Chang-Hoon, Lee, "Heuristic-based Approach for Phishing

Site Detection Using URL Features " in the proceedings of the third international conference

on Advances in Computing, Electronics and Electrical Technology - CEET 2015,USA,

April,2015.[16]

34. Justin Ma , Lawrence K. Saul , Stefan Savage , Geoffrey M. Voelker," Learning to Detect

Malicious URLs ", ACM Transactions on Intelligent Systems and Technology, Vol. 2,

No. 3, Article 30,April 2011.[17]

35. Justin Ma, Lawrence K.Saul, Stefan Savage, Geoffrey M. Volker. "Identifying Suspicious

URLs: An Application of Large-Scale Online Learning". Proceedings of the 26th Annual

International Conference on Machine Learning. ACM NewYork, NY USA 2009. [18]

DOI:10.1145/1553374.1553462.

36. Justin Ma , Lawrence K. Saul , Stefan Savage , Geoffrey M. Voelker, Beyond blacklists:

learning to detect malicious web sites from suspicious URLs, Proceedings of the 15th

ACM SIGKDD international conference on knowledge discovery and data mining, June 28-

July 01, 2009, Paris, France.DOI:10.1145/1557019.1557153[19].

37.M. Khonji, Y. Iraqi, and A. Jones, "Phishing detection: a literature survey," IEEE

Communications Surveys & Tutorials, vol. 15, no. 4,pp. 2091–2121, 2013.[35]

38.P. Kolari, T. Finin, and A. Joshi, "Svms for the blogosphere: Blog identification and splog

detection," in AAAI Spring Symposium: Computational Approaches to Analyzing Weblogs,

2006, pp. 92–99.[57]

39. C. Kolbitsch, B. Livshits, B. Zorn, and C. Seifert, "Rozzle: De-cloaking internet

malware," in Security and Privacy (SP), 2012 IEEE Symposium on. IEEE, 2012, pp. 443–

457.[42]

40.M. Kuyama, Y. Kakizaki, and R. Sasaki, "Method for detecting a malicious domain by using

whois and dns features," in The Third International Conference on Digital Security and

Forensics (DigitalSec2016), 2016, p. 74.[67]

41.A. Le, A. Markopoulou, and M. Faloutsos, "Phishdef: Url names say it all," in INFOCOM,

2011 Proceedings IEEE. IEEE, 2011, pp. 191–195.[47]

42. M.S. Lin, C.-Y. Chiu, Y.-J. Lee, and H.-K. Pao, "Malicious url filteringa big data

application," in Big Data, 2013 IEEE International Conference on. IEEE, 2013, pp. 589–596.

[39]

43.W. Liu, X. Deng, G. Huang, and A. Y. Fu, "An antiphishing strategy based on visual

similarity assessment," IEEE Internet Computing, vol. 10, no. 2, p. 58, 2006.[60]

44. F. Maggi, A. Frossi, S. Zanero, G. Stringhini, B. Stone-Gross, C. Kruegel, and G. Vigna,

"Two years of short urls internet measurement: security threats and countermeasures," in

Proceedings of the 22nd international conference on World Wide Web. International World

Wide Web Conferences Steering Committee, 2013, pp. 861–872.[61]

45. Manuel Egele , Theodoor Scholte , Engin Kirda , Christopher Kruegel, A survey on

automated dynamic malware-analysis techniques and tools, ACM Computing Surveys

(CSUR), v.44 n.2, p.1-42, February 2012.[20]

46. Marie Vasek and Tyler Moore,"Empirical analysis of factors affecting malware URL

Detection" in 8th APWG eCrime Researchers Summit (eCrime), September 2013.[21]

47. D. K. McGrath and M. Gupta, "Behind phishing: An examination of phisher modi operandi,"

In Proc. of the USENIX Workshop on Large- Scale Exploits and Emergent Threats(LEET),

San Francisco, CA, 2008.[22]

48.Mitsuaki Akiyama, Takeshi Yagi, Takeshi Yada, Tatsuya Mori, Youki Kadobayashi,

Analyzing the ecosystem of malicious URL redirection through longitudinal observation from

honeypots, computers & security (2017), doi: 10.1016/j.cose.2017.01.003.[48]

49. Monther Aldwairi , Rami Alsalman, "MALURLS: A lightweight Malicious Website

Classification Based on URL Features", Journal of Emerging Technologies in Web

Intelligence (JETWI), Vol. 4, No. 2, pp.128-133, 2012. [23]

50. Onashoga, S. A.,, Abayomi-Alli,, A., Idowu, O., Okesola, J. O",A Hybrid Approach

for Detecting Malicious Web Pages Using Decision Tree and Navie Bayes Algorithm",

Georgian Electronic Scientific Journal: Computer Science and

Telecommunications,No.2(48),2016.[24]

51. D. R. Patil and J. Patil, "Survey on malicious web pages detection techniques," International

Journal of u-and e-Service, Science and Technology, vol. 8, no. 5, pp. 195–206, 2015. [66].

52. Pete Burnap, Amir Javed, Omer F. Rana, Malik S. Awan "Real-time Classification of

Malicious URLs on Twitter using Machine Activity Data", Proceeding of the 2015

IEEE/ACM International Conference on Advances in Social Networks Analysis and

Mining.August 25-28, 2015, Paris, France DOI:

http://dx.doi.org/10.1145/2808797.2809281.[25]

53.P. Prakash, M. Kumar, R. R. Kompella, and M. Gupta, "Phishnet: predictive blacklisting to

detect phishing attacks," in INFOCOM, 2010 Proceedings IEEE. IEEE, 2010, pp. 1–5. [43]

54. Prasse, P., Gruben, G., Machlika, L., Pevny, T., Sofka, M., & Scheffer, T. (2017). Malware

Detection by HTTPS Traffic Analysis.published at the Institutional Repository of the

Potsdam University.2017.[69]

55. Provos, N., Mavrommatis, P., Rajab, M. A., Monrose, F., July 2008. All your iframes point

to us. In: Proceeding of the 17th conference on USENIX Security Symposium (USENIX

SS'08). San Jose, CA, USA, pp. 1–15.[26]

56. PHISHTANK. Open DNS project available at http://www.phishtank.com

57. Ram B. Basnet , Andrew H. Sung , Quingzhong Liu," Learning to Detect Malicious

URLs", International Journal of Research in Engineering and Technology, Volume: 03 Issue:

06,ISSN: 2319-1163, June 2014.[27]

58. Romil Rawat Megha Zodape Praveen kataria chandrapal singh dangi," URLAD (URL attack

detection) - using SVM", International Journal of Advanced Research in Computer Science

and Software Engineering,,Volume 2, Issue 1, ISSN 2277-128X, January 2012.[28]

59. Ms. Roshani K. Chaudhari, Prof. D. M. Dakhane ,"A Review on Enhanced Machine

Learning Approach for Detection of Malicious Urls and Spam in Social

Network", International Journal of Advanced Research in Computer Engineering &

Technology (IJARCET), Volume 5 Issue 2, February 2016. [29]

60. Saurabh Muthal,Ameya Pawar, Saurabh Harne,"A Hybrid Approach to Detect Suspicious

URLs",Vol-2 Issue-2 2016, International Journal of Advanced Research and Innovative Ideas

in Education,Volume -2 Issue-2 2016.[30]

61. Schiavoni S, Maggi F, Cavallaro L, Zanero S. Phoenix: DGA-based botnet tracking and

intelligence. In: Proceedings of the 11th international conference on detection of intrusions

and malware, and vulnerability assessment (DIMVA); 2014.[50]

62. E. Sorio, A. Bartoli, and E. Medvet, "Detection of hidden fraudulent urls within trusted sites

using lexical features," in Availability, Reliability and Security (ARES), 2013 Eighth

International Conference on.IEEE, 2013, pp. 242–247.[52]

63.SPOORTHI K ,SARVAMANGALA D R ,"Mail_Alert: Online Suspicious URL Detection of

Tweets from Twitter Public Timeline", , International Journal of Computer Science and

Mobile Computing, Vol.3 Issue.4, April- 2014, pp. 817-824.[31]

64.G. Stringhini, C. Kruegel, and G. Vigna, "Shady paths: Leveraging surfing crowds to detect

malicious web pages," in Proceedings of the 2013 ACM SIGSAC conference on Computer &

communications security. ACM, 2013, pp. 133–144.[64]

65.B. Sun, M. Akiyama, T. Yagi, M. Hatada, and T. Mori, "Autoblg: Automatic url blacklist

generator using search space expansion and filters," in 2015 IEEE Symposium on Computers

and Communication (ISCC). IEEE, 2015, pp. 625–631.[36]

66.Tammo Krueger and Konrad Rieck. Intelligent defense against malicious javascript code.PIK

Praxis der Informationsverarbeitung und Kommunikation, 35(1):54-60, 2012.

DOI 10.1515/pik-2012-0009.[32][37]

.

68. K. Thomas, C. Grier, J. Ma, V. Paxson, and D. Song, "Design and evaluation of a real-time

url spam filtering service," in Security andPrivacy (SP), 2011 IEEE Symposium on. IEEE,

2011, pp. 447–462.[63]

69. L. Wenyin, G. Huang, L. Xiaoyue, Z. Min, and X. Deng, "Detection of phishing webpages

based on visual similarity," in Special interest tracks and posters of the 14th international

conference on World Wide Web. ACM, 2005, pp. 1060–1061.[59]

70. S. Yadav, A. K. K. Reddy, A. Reddy, and S. Ranjan, "Detecting algorithmically generated

malicious domain names," in Proceedings of the 10th ACM SIGCOMM conference on

Internet measurement. ACM, 2010, pp. 48–61.[38]

71.W. Zhang, Y.-X. Ding, Y. Tang, and B. Zhao, "Malicious web page detection based on on-

line learning algorithm," in Machine Learning and Cybernetics (ICMLC), 2011 International

Conference on, vol. 4. IEEE, 2011, pp. 1914–1919.[46]

72. Y. Zhang, J. I. Hong, and L. F. Cranor, "Cantina: a content-based approach to detecting

phishing web sites," in Proceedings of the 16th international conference on World Wide Web.

ACM, 2007, pp. 639–648.[54]

www.ingramcontent.com/pod-product-compliance
Lightning Source LLC
LaVergne TN
LVHW050419160726
843469LV00041B/1147

9789356105416